Poems by Revelation

By

Dr. Lydia A. Woods

†††
CWP

Channing & Watt Publishers
Peoria, AZ

First Edition, Copyright @ 1995
Second Edition, Copyright @ 2014

Printed in the United States of America

ISBN-13: 978-1-941200-13-1

LCCN: 2014930487

Other Publications
by Dr. Lydia A. Woods

Acceptance with Joy
For the Edification of the Saints
Food for Saints
Let Those with Ears…
Conversations with the Saints
All the Saints Agree
Those Bible Women
Those Bible Characters
Made in the Fire
The Joy of the Lord
Under the Rainbow

Dedicated to

My Parents with Love
Mildred and Charles Woods

Acknowledgements

A piece of creative work is usually produced in isolation, but the distribution for others to see and appreciate takes many hearts and hands and minds. I want to give thanks to my friends and family members who are those hearts which support and lift me up and forward.

Special thanks to William C. Terry, Yehonatan Meru, and Veronica Norris for taking their time to proofread this book.

My appreciation to the host of colleagues, students and fellow Christian brothers and sisters who praise and encourage me and constantly remind me of the work God can do in a willing but frightened and fragile vessel.

Thank you, Holy Spirit, for using my humble vessel
and letting me put my name on these words.

Introduction

Under the inspiration of the Holy Spirit, I began writing Christian Poetry. The Spirit would "overshadow" me as the old folk used to say and I would copy down what was given. The Spirit would leave and return again several months later. This continued for about five years until there was enough poetry for me to begin questioning the Lord as to the purpose of this gift. He instructed me to begin to put the poems all in one place in an orderly format. The first book, entitled "Poems by Revelation," was the result. While putting the book in publishable form the Spirit became extremely active which led to a second collection of poems and thus, I began on the unlikely path of author/publisher.

These collections of poems are inspired by the lessons which the Lord has been teaching me over years of walking with Him. Many poems are inspired by uplifting and stimulating conversations with God's precious saints and others are born out of frustration from ungodliness and ignorance of God's Word which exist around me.

In reading, I hope you will find poems which speak to your heart and express what you have experienced on your walk with the Father. The writing of these poems allows me an outlet of expression as the Lord tempers and prepares me for my calling.

Table of Contents

Poems

Scriptural References

Poems

Dr. Lydia A. Woods

A Bible Character

Luke 22:47, 57, 60; 23:21-34; Mark 15:1, 10-11, 16:1;
Matthew 21:24; 1 Peter 2:9 (KJV)
Scriptural Reference on page 47

I've heard the Holy Book called the, "Living Word,"
It lives and breathes, and strains to be heard.
And I heard a Saint say, I'd like to be,
A Bible character for all to see.

No sooner said, than the chance came their way,
The Word leapt from the page to the everyday.
And all of a sudden that Word came alive,
The Holy Spirit had heard, and opportunity arrived.

It's an honor to be on the battlefield,
In the perilous days when warfare is real.
We'll all get our chance to stand for Christ,
And prove to everyone that we're bought with a price.

Which character will you be on that Bible stage,
If the casting is done and war is waged?
Are you Judas, who comes with kisses by night,
Or Pilate who washes the blood out of sight?

Are you in the crowd crying crucify Him,
Or Peter who denies that he is His friend?
Or the soldiers who cast lots for His garment in greed
Or the wicked leaders who arranged the deed?

Are you one of the twelve who walked with Him,
But couldn't be found when the evening grew dim?
Were you one of the women, He delivered from sin,
But remembered that He said, "He would rise again?"

Even though they were afraid, they went to the tomb,
To give honor to their Lord and His body groom.
Will you be counted with the very few,
Who waited on the Lord as their hope grew?

And believed all He'd said would come true,
That He would return for me and you.
And in the meantime, while we're on earth,
Washed in His blood, a child of new birth.

Just check yourself out in every way,
And see which role you'll play today.
Could they cast you for peculiar people indeed,
The Royal Priesthood and Child of His seed?

Called by His name and set aside,
The Temple of God, let His Spirit abide.
In the beauty of Holiness tried and true,
Let His Spirit be found in me and you.

A Bible Character

Birthright

Genesis 27:1-46; 28:1-22 (KJV)
Scriptural Reference on page 50

The story of Jacob and Esau is over the top,
I started reading about them and could not stop.
You should check it out when I am through,
'Cause it will speak, I'm sure, directly to you!

I bet you didn't know that they were twins,
Jacob was second to come out, so Esau did win.
The right to inherit all his father's wealth and land,
Jacob was on the out – but his mother had a plan.

Jacob was her favorite son you see,
She wanted Jacob to inherit, but this is the key.
Isaac's blessing would go only to the one,
Who would inherit – Esau the favorite son.

So, she plotted to get that blessing you know,
And Jacob helped in the deception just so.
He got his brother to sell his birthright for food,
Now taking his brother's birthright was a bit rude.

They were very different these twins indeed,
One was smooth the other hairy – now take heed.
How could Jacob fool this blind old man,
He would know when he touched Jacob's hand.

So, he covered his hands and neck with fur skins,
It did the trick, and the blessing Jacob did win.
His brother's blessing he took in a flash,
Forever his – and that blessing would last.

Esau hated his brother for what he had done,
He swore to kill him – put Jacob on the run.
Now you know what goes around comes again,
Jacob's treachery would visit him in the end.

And so, it did in a far-off land,
He fell in love with the daughter of his Uncle Laban.
He worked seven years to win her hand,
But on the wedding night Laban had a plan.

He tricked Jacob and put Leah in his bed,
And bargained seven more years before he could wed,
His beloved Rachel – so the trick was done,
But more grief to Jacob was waiting to come.

Rachel couldn't have that precious child,
Trouble was stirring in this marriage all the while.
Jacob had ten sons before his favorite came,
Rachel finally had a son and Joseph was his name.

So, remember when you set out to do no good,
It just comes rolling back seven-fold as it should.
God will give you all your blessings indeed,
Don't take someone else's in your greed.

Birthright

Dr. Lydia A. Woods

Bringing His Family Out

Genesis 3:22-24; Mark 1:14-15; 1 Peter 2:9; 1 Corinthians 2:12; Ephesians 1:3-6; Acts 2:17; Matthew 24:21-22; Hebrews 10:38 (KJV)
Scriptural Reference on page 55

My beloved, there's a secret I'll reveal to you,
Of God's glorious plan tried and true.
You remember of old, how Adam fell,
And condemned us all to eternal hell?

God turned His face from man that day,
The sin we bore made Him put us away.
Satan didn't know God was a step ahead,
And had a plan for him and his final bed.

God's precious Son said that He would go,
Into the world and let the people know,
Of the Father's love, and of His life-giving Word.
Of which the world had never really heard.

Of His glorious Kingdom Jesus testified,
And the people knew that the Pharisee's had lied.
God wanted a people to call His own,
Who would follow His Word, into the unknown.

And walk by faith - blind - without natural sight,
But would trust in Him with all their might.
A peculiar people to the world they would be,
But this sets us apart both you and me.

Bringing His Family Out

We're a race of beings that has never been before,
Born of the Spirit that come to God by just one door.
Through the blood of His Son, His family shines pure,
The Righteousness of God of that I am sure.

We are scattered in the world called by name,
Joined by One Spirit which makes us the same.
Brothers and sisters laborers in the field,
Working to increase God's family yield.

His Holy Spirit is the key to unlocking the truth,
With revelation knowledge you'll have the proof,
That we are living in perilous times, these last days,
So live by faith and truth in all your ways.

It won't be long, then we'll be homeward bound,
The signs of this are all around.
God's plan is being fulfilled as I speak,
Keep the faith, be strong, steadfast not weak.

God has shortened the time for the Elects' sake,
Jesus is coming soon with Saints in His wake.
God's glorious plan is working like a charm,
He's bringing His family out by His mighty arm.

Bringing His Family Out

Dr. Lydia A. Woods

The Day of His Birth

Genesis 1:26-27; Luke 2:6-14 (KJV)
Scriptural Reference on page 57

The Lord created man from the dust of the earth,
He breathed life into him and gave him birth.

He gave him dominion and power beyond compare,
But man betrayed His trust, on Satan's dare.

But the Lord was ready with plans of His own,
To bring His Son to earth from His golden throne.

He was born in a manger on Christmas day,
There was no room in the inn, so the scriptures say.

Three came to worship Him from near and far,
They were guided by the light of the brightest star.

Three wise men brought Him incense, myrrh, and gold,
The shepherds left their flocks as they were told.

The Heavenly Host did sing of His new Birth,
Of Good Will Toward Men and Peace on Earth.

Dr. Lydia A. Woods

Doin' the Israelite

Exodus 11:2, 13:21, 14:27-28, 16:2-3,12, 17:2-4 (KJV)
Scriptural Reference on page 58

Have you ever thought after reading about,
How the Lord brought the Israelites out?
Just how they could murmur and complain,
It boggles my mind and spins my brain.

I call it, "Doin' the Israelite!"

I couldn't imagine after all God had done,
Wanting to turn back high-tail-it and run.
Back to bondage and the Pharaoh's whip,
And not wanting to make that glorious trip.

I call it, "Doin' the Israelite!"

After bringing them out with silver and gold,
Every man, woman, child from the young to the old.
After parting the sea and walking on dry land,
And destroying the enemy with a sweep of his hand.

I call it, "Doin' the Israelite!"

How could they slip back to their ungodly way,
While Moses was getting what God had to say.
On the tablets of stone Gods' glorious Word,
Of which his people had never heard.

I call it, "Doin' the Israelite!"

Now remember how He led them by night and by day,
Leading them so evident all of the way.
And all of the miracles and the wondrous feats,
Water from stone and manna to eat.

I call it, "Doin' the Israelite!"

He kept them better than the birds or the lilies of the field,
It's hard to comprehend, it can't really be real,
But now as I take my wilderness walk,
Sometimes I have to check my thoughts and my talk.

Am I, "Doin' the Israelite?"

I find that, I too, murmur and complain,
And sometimes I think I'll go insane.
I know the Spirit of God dwells in me,
And I should walk by faith unable to see.

Am I, "Doin' the Israelite?"

It isn't as easy, as it looks,
I thought it would be, after reading his book.
His account of the Israelites warns all of us,
Of the possible fate if we doubt and mistrust.

Are you, "Doin' the Israelite?"

Saints, believe what I'm about to say,
You will do the Israelite every day.
Yes, I'm telling it right and telling it straight,
We are all filled, with fear, mistrust, and hate.

Are you, "Doin' the Israelite?"

Lord, help and forgive me, I repent and ask,
For strength and understanding, so I can last.
The entire way to the Promise land,
Don't leave me in the wilderness, bring me out by your hand.

I don't want to be caught, "Doin' the Israelite!"

Doin' the Israelite

Lord I want to be found steadfast and true,
Faithful to the end, believing in you.
You never said, it would be easy or a piece of cake,
But that tribulation would come, and it's for our sakes.

I'm growing in faith every day,
I believe you'll perfect me in every way.
But it's not because I am so good,
Or because I have faith like I should.

But because you are faithful and true to your word,
And what you have started, you'll finish, I've heard.
And in the end, everything will be right,
And I won't be caught, "Doin' the Israelite!"

Get a Testimony

Luke 4:18-19; James 1:2-4 (KJV)
Scriptural Reference on page 60

The Lord showed me a truth some time ago,
When I was just reborn about a month or so.

To testify of the Father Jesus came,
To make known His Kingdom and to proclaim,
Of what He knew to be the truth of His Father's love.
And to send the Holy Spirit to us like a dove.

Well, it dawned on me what was going on,
Our walk with God is no different from His Son's!
Our mission like His is the same for me and you,
We need to proclaim what we know of the Father too.

How can we do that if not for tribulation and trial,
So a personal witness we become, our testimony to compile.
For the testimony as the Lord explained it to me.
Is Anointed from above, speak it out and see.

Now there are certain ones that the Lord will send on your path.
It's time to tell your testimony that's really your task.
It's not for everyone you meet,
But to those whom the Father sends - it is so sweet.

They will be edified and surely lifted up.
As the anointing flows and they drink from that cup.
You know for a fact of what He's done for you.
How you overcame, and He saw you through.

Once you are born again, and tribulation comes,
You begin to make that testimony one by one.
You have so many miracles of what He's done for you,
You can't even count them if you tried to.

When I think about all He's done on my walk,
I get real happy and just talk and talk.
I experience a feeling of elevation,
My spirit soars with pure elation.

Sometimes I testify well into the night,
My spirit is renewed and filled with delight.
I am floating three feet above the floor.
I just want to talk about Him more and more.

This feeling lasts long after I am through,
Are you listening well 'cause I'm talking to you.
So get yourself a testimony of the Father's Love.
Get on the job, your orders are straight from above.

Get yourself a testimony, not someone else's, you see,
Yours is Anointed for you, and you're in good company.
For Jesus testified of the father and what He knew,
We each have our own and there's one waiting for you!

Get a Testimony

Getting to Know You

Proverbs 1:7, 2:1,3:1-4 (KJV)
Scriptural Reference on page 61

Lord, it's been a joy just getting to know You,
Through the hard times, when You carried me through.
Our friendship has grown and blossomed over the years.
Through it all You've eased my mind and calmed my fears.

Your nature is sweet and loving and kind,
Your patience with me, sometimes blows my mind.
We have a special relationship, You and me,
It's something that no one else can see.

Your Spirit speaks to mine throughout the day,
I'm not always listening to what You have to say.
I get caught up in the cares of this crazy world,
And sometimes my flesh keeps my mind in a whirl.

Then You remind me of what Your Word said,
About renewing my mind, not relying on my own head.
Walking by the Spirit and not by sight,
Living every day without fear or fright,

Of what tomorrow will bring or what the bill collectors' say,
But letting You guide my footsteps day by day.
I'm better today than yesterday and further along this path,
I'm holding on to faith and enduring to the last.

Where I am weak You are very strong,
Through You, I can do all things, I can't go wrong.
I'm practicing resting in You with every trial,
I know Your work in me will take a while.

I can see the changes as I look back,
That's what keeps me going, steady on this track.
I have tasted of Your goodness, it's fine and sweet.
I'm looking forward to when face to face we meet.

I hope it won't be long, please don't tarry Dear,
I'll be ready and waiting, for the Bridegroom here.
In a place that is not my real true home,
Take me back to the life where I belong.

Where peace and joy are ever present there,
Where angels sing Your praises and everyone will share.
In glorifying the Father and Son both day and night,
And Love will abound, and all things will finally be right.

Getting to Know You

Good News

*1 Corinthians 15:3, 15:52; Mark 13:24-27; Revelation 1:7, 19:7-9, 20:1-3,
21:1-5 (KJV) Scriptural Reference on page 62*

Jesus died on the cross, for our souls,
He took our sickness in His body, so it was told.

That's how it all began a long time ago,
I'm not telling no tales that you don't know.

Brothers and sisters, you better listen up,
And take a long cool drink from the Jesus cup.

It's time we all got saved, in these terrible times,
You know the rapture's comin', don't be left behind.

He's comin' in the clouds, in a twinkle of an eye,
You know the Saints that are living, will not die.

So, believe in Him and in the power of His might,
'Cause He's coming like a thief, in the night.

And then there's seven long years, of hell on earth,
It's the tribulation times, Thank God for His Birth!

'Cause the Saints will be rockin' at the marriage feast,
And those here on earth will be fighting the beast.

Now He's coming back to set up His reign,
The earth will be changed, it won't be the same.

We're all coming back as Kings and Priest,
We won't have to contend with the beast.

He'll be sitting in the pit, with all of his gang,
Until Jesus is finished with His thousand-year reign.

Then Satan watch out cause yo' end is near,
The lake of fire is what you fear.

Now I'm telling the truth of what the scriptures say,
There's a Holy New Jerusalem on its way.

God will dwell with men on this new earth,
No sorrow will exist in this new birth.

So, get your heart right and set your mind,
And get Salvation now and put your sins behind.

I'm spreading the Good News throughout the Land,
That Jesus Christ, He is our man!
That Jesus Christ, He is our man!
That Jesus Christ, He is our man!

Good News

Good News II

Mark 16:15-18; Revelation 2:1-29, 3:1-22 (KJV)
Scriptural Reference on page 64

I've got more Good News, in Good News II,
For years you sat in church, on that cold, hard pew.
The preacher ranted and raved about repenting from sin,
But never told of the Glory you would win.

I'm here to "Shout the Good News" at the top of my lungs,
And tell about all the good things you have won.

When Jesus did His thing on the cross that day,
He took the sins of the world forever away.
He took your sickness in His body, so get off your bed,
Get it down, in your spirit, just what I said.

God could turn His face to man again,
The Blood of His Son washed away all sin.
He could hear the cries of a world He created,
And begin His family for so long He had waited.

To institute an adoption plan,
And pass His Holy Spirit to His recreated Man.

Now Jesus rose from the dead to sit at the right hand,
A Priest that intercedes between God and Man.
Jesus had to die, to give a new testament,
And rise again, an inheritance to present.

So, use the name of Jesus to cast the devil out,
Lay your hands on the sick and never doubt.
Eat any deadly thing it won't hurt you,
Raise the dead to life, as you were told to do.

Cause when He poured His Spirit out on you,
You became a new creature, with work to do!!
Into all the world to tell of His glory,
But that's not the end of this precious story.

BELOVED!!

I'm telling the truth of what the scriptures say,
There's a Holy new Jerusalem on its way.
God will dwell with men on this new earth,
No sorrow will exist in this new birth.

So, get your heart right, and set your mind,
Get Salvation now and put your sins behind.
I'm spreading the Good News, throughout the Land,
That Jesus Christ is still our Man!
That Jesus Christ is still our Man!
That Jesus Christ is still our Man!

Good News II

It's Adoption Time

Galatians 4:5-7; Ephesians 1:4-5 (KJV)
Scriptural Reference on page 70

Man's law states that you may not abuse,
The little children, and if you're accused,
And found to misuse your parental authority,
A new Family will be found for the children, you see.

That was God's plan first, not man's you know,
For we were kidnapped from God, so long ago.
The evil deed took place in the garden that day,
And we grew-up believing what the devil had to say.

We thought he was our father, you see,
But the kidnapper had no love for you or me,
He only came to kill, and steal and destroy,
To take away our birthright and steal our joy.

But just like, in the world, in the orphanage,
A plan is set up for the unfortunate,
That's God's plan for us, from heaven above.
To take those children who have never known love.

Each orphan is waiting to be called by name,
To a family belong and be rid of the shame.
To be rescued from the pain and the grief,
Resting in their Father's arms, in grace and peace.

Wait no more the paperwork is done,
When Jesus died on the cross the victory was won.
For His brothers and sisters a way was made,
All who live by His Word, will surely be saved.

It's adoption time, no more abuse to bear,
It won't be long that the prince of the air,
Will get his just desserts, for his child abuse,
Just read the Holy Word don't be obtuse.

Little children come into His family and accept His love,
It's freely given to you from God above.

From death to life, you'll be born again,
Washed in His Blood, a stranger to sin.
You'll grow in grace every day in every way,
Surely goodness and mercy will follow you that day.

When you take Christ to be your Lord and King,
He'll make your song sweet and you will sing,
Of His grace and glory and mercy and truth,
I'm an Adoptive child of God, I am living proof.

It's Adoption Time

It's War!

Ephesians 6:10-17 (KJV)
Scriptural Reference on page 71

It's War!
When you take Jesus and you're reborn,
There's something you should know that's going on.

It's War!
In high places that you can't see,
Put on your Spiritual ears, and listen to me.

It's War!
Yeah, it's war, that I'm talking about,
When I am finished there will be no doubt.

It's War!
Against darkness and wickedness on high,
If you listen real well there's no fear you'll die!

It's War!
But the victory's yours, without a doubt,
Your Savior fought the fight and worked it all out.

It's War!
But there is a special way you fight,
You just stand still with all of your might.

It's War!
And there's a special armor you wear,
The helmet of Salvation won't muss your hair.

And on your loins the Truth you'll wear,
The Breastplate of Righteousness won't even tear.

You have the Gospel of Peace upon your feet,
And with the Shield in hand you won't feel the heat,

From the wicked fiery darts being thrown at you,
You don't have to despair, you know what to do.

With the Sword in hand just lift it high,
And quench those darts and watch them fly.

But you're not hurt, you only have to stand,
And be very patient and wait on your Man.

Cause He's coming in a cloud to rescue you,
The Holy One of God, Tried and True.

It's War!
And you're commanded to watch and pray,
I can hear the Lord say on that final day,

Well done good soldier - come on in,
Did you have a doubt that we would win?

And in the end, you'll be proud to say,
I had my armor on and withstood the evil day.

It's War!

Joseph

Genesis 37:2-5, 9, 15, 31-35, 41:41-43, 45:1-5 (KJV)
Scriptural Reference on page 72

In the Bible there are people whose stories are told,
I know you think they're outdated and very old.
But there's a lesson to learn for us today,
Let me lay it out in a simple way.

Now take Joseph for instance and what happened to him,
All those brothers who threw him over the rim
Of that deep dark pit, then plotted his demise,
Joseph hadn't acted cool or very wise.

Jacob loved Joseph more than the others,
This caused a lot of hate in Joseph's brothers.
And beside all that, he made Joseph that coat,
It really made the brothers mad and got their goat.

But that's not all, there's a little more,
Joseph had those dreams, so the brothers evened the score.
Into slavery they sold Joseph on that day,
Dipped the coat in blood and to Jacob did say,

That a wild beast had torn him from limb to limb,
Jacob mourned and grieved for his future was dim,
Cause his precious son was gone never to return,
He rent his clothes - his kin were very concerned.

They could not comfort him, all the daughters and sons,
And that's how Joseph's long journey had begun.

Joseph went through trials and tribulations galore,
He was lied on, thrown in prison, I know his heart was sore.
He missed his father and even those brothers, you see,
He had years to work out resentment, to set his soul free.

All through the bad times he held onto his God,
His masters thought him strange and very odd.
But God watched over Joseph for he had a plan,
To bring all Jacob's children to Goshen land.

Well, the day finally came and face to face they came,
Joseph and his brothers - my how Joseph had changed.
Pharaoh had set Joseph over his house and lands,
To keep them all from starving, just a part of God's plan.

Not only had Joseph changed, but the brothers too,
Joseph tested them, he gave them back their due.
They repented for the evil deed done so long ago,
But God turned it to their good, don't you know.

For that's the secret I'm about to reveal to you,
There is one in each family that God works through.
For the Salvation of the others it's a glorious plan,
Are you the one that God has cut out with His hand?

Are you the odd one, that never seems to fit in?
Praying for Salvation of all your family in the end.
Calling on the name of the Lord every day,
On your wilderness walk not seeing your way?

Joseph

Well take heart 'cause it's all promised to you,
God will honor His Word and see your family through.
Like Joseph He'll set you on high with His Son,
He'll raise you up after you have done.

Your appointed time in the wilderness,
As you cling to your God and sin resist.
See those stories aren't so old for us today,
Take heart and let them encourage you on your way!

Just Do It!

Mark 16:15-20 (KJV)
Scriptural Reference on page 74

These signs shall follow them that believe,
Come on Saints, I know that you can read.
I found these signs in Mark sixteen and seventeen,
I didn't read about this in any comic magazine!

It says, to use His name to cast the devil out,
Don't you think that's what Saints should be about?
Jesus cast the devil out while He walked among us,
We should use His name, not fear spirits and trust.

That His Word is true, and there is power in His name,
Keep working that Word you won't be the same.
Now at first it might not look like you're doing a thing,
But in the spirit world you've created a scene.

You have rocked the house of where Satan lives,
Keep using the name until Satan gives.
Just keep it up and don't think to quit,
'Cause you're commanded to.

"Just Do It!"

It also says, with new tongues they will speak,
So get your new tongue, get power, don't be weak.
Tongues edify you not anyone else, you see,
It's evidence of the Holy Spirit in thee.

It's a gift you ask for so make that choice,
Open up your mouth and give the Holy Spirit a voice.
Praying in the Spirit is a more perfect way,
To fulfill what He's commanded us to do every day.

It also builds that faith, and this pleases God,
I know it sounds kind of funny and you look odd.
But remember you're a peculiar people indeed.
Born of His Spirit a child of His seed.

Don't be concerned about how you look,
'Cause it's written in His Holy Book.
Just keep it up and don't think to quit,
'Cause you're commanded to.

"Just Do It!"

It also says, to heal the sick,
Lay hands on them the healing is quick.
How many Saints have you seen doing this?
It doesn't take special gifts there is no risk.

They will talk about you, and probably laugh out loud,
While you are imitating the Son all the while.
Can you stand to look strange and face the doubt?
But remember that's what peculiar people are all about.

Now at first it might not look like you're doing a thing,
But in the spirit world you've created a scene.
You remind the devil that he can't stay,
He has to honor the Word and be on his way.

You have rocked the house of where Satan lives,
Keep using the name until Satan gives.
Just keep it up and don't think to quit,
'Cause' you're commanded to.

"Just Do it!"

Just Do It!

Master of Masters

Matthew 4:1, 4:19, 5:1, 7:29, 8:26, 11:5; Luke 8:43-48;
John 2:1-11, 11:43-44 (KJV)
Scriptural Reference on page 75

The Master of Masters was a fisher of men,
He taught the people and forgave all their sin.
He was tempted of Satan in the wilderness,
But full of the Spirit He did resist.

He was pressed by the multitude from all around,
On the mountain He taught, and made the Word profound.
He delivered the sick from all their pain,
He broke down the law and made it plain.

He made the blind to see and He calmed the rain,
And healed the minds of those insane.
He turned the water to wine, at the wedding feast,
He sent foul, filthy spirits into the beast.

A woman with faith who believed in Him,
And did not believe her chances were dim.
Touched the hem of His garment and she got blessed,
And captured the virtue He did possess.

Now it's written all there in His Holy Book,
Just open it up and have a look.
He raised the dead to life, and made the lame to walk,
He spent time with His disciples, and they did talk.

About eternal life and the Father above,
And of that greatest commandment - How to Love.
He spoke in parables, so only they would know,
The ones with ears, could learn and grow.

Who open their hearts, and the Son accept,
And repent of their sins, which gives Him respect.
Cause He's the Master of Masters, the Holy One,
The Alpha and Omega, God's Beloved Son.

Master of Masters

Dr. Lydia A. Woods

No Abundance in the Wilderness

Matthew 4:1-11 (KJV)
Scriptural Reference on page 78

Take heed Saints, I'll not have you ignorant,
Some of us are in the midst of the wilderness,
We shouldn't expect every comfort or plenty,
For in the wilderness there isn't any.

In the wilderness all that can be found,
Is the Grace of the Savior we adore.
Teaching each of His precious children,
To depend on Him more and more.

In the wilderness we must become as little children,
Dependent on Him for every need.
Learning to live in a world,
Filled with jealousy, hatred, and greed.

In the wilderness you won't be quite alone,
Other children of God are also there too.
When we meet, we encourage each other,
Lifting spirits and our strength renew.

The Lord commanded the Israelites gather the manna,
So they gathered according to each need,
God spoiled it when they tried to store up,
And gathered too much in their greed.

God wanted the Israelites to depend on Him,
Every day and in all of their ways,
Becoming a peculiar people not like any other race.
Looking to him and seeking only His Face.

Don't try to store up treasures and material things,
Putting aside for that rainy day,
Naming it and claiming it with money to spare.
For we must completely place ourselves in His care.

For God wants to prove to us His love,
The wilderness experience is the perfect place.
Ever mindful that without Him we're not complete,
Teaching us to be humble, and without self-deceit.

For when Jesus left the wilderness after 40 days,
His ministry spread throughout the land,
He began to preach the gospel of the Kingdom,
He died and rose again for the Salvation of Man.

So, when your wilderness experience is complete,
How strong and steadfast your faith will be,
You'll be rooted and grounded in the Lord,
Prepared for your ministry, not bound, completely free.

So, the wilderness is just for a season,
Our needs will be met, and we'll surely be blessed,
A training period to develop faith in the Lord,
But remember, "There's No Abundance in the Wilderness."

No Abundance in the Wilderness

Put It All On!

Ephesians 6:11-17 (KJV)
Scriptural Reference on page 79

God said, to put the whole armor on,
It's the gift you get when you're reborn.

Now you probably heard it many times before,
To put it on - don't let Satan in the door.

It's not too big, it fits just right,
'Cause you can't fight in your own might.

The Lord wants you to be able to stand,
In the evil day and take command,

Over Satan's wickedness - put him under your feet,
It'll give you pleasure; the victory is sweet.

Have you ever thought, what would happen to you,
If you didn't obey, what God told you to do?

That's why many Saints today are laying down,
And pieces of the armor are scattered around.

'Cause they just don't know how to keep it on,
Even though they've been saved and are reborn.

Unless it's all on, you won't have success,
You get attacked and your life's a mess.

Those wicked fiery darts keep coming fast,
At times you feel that you won't last.

Just check yourself out, a piece is slipping down,
And before you know it, Satan's got you bound.

So, keep the helmet on, your mind to protect,
Darts are aimed there, so you'll lose respect,

For the Word of God and His integrity,
Satan wants to take your joy, so your peace will flee.

And when peace is gone it's confusion there,
Some armor is missing, and you're in despair.

So, renew your mind everyday -
Wash it with the Word, so you can say,

"It is written Satan -- Get behind me,"
Experience the Power of the Word and watch him flee!

Put It All On!

Quest for Salvation

Malachi 3:13-18 (KJV)
Scriptural Reference on page 80

We've been round and round with this old thing,
Look at the sorrow that the Quest for Salvation brings.
Every quest has its ups and downs,
Even the road to Salvation where I am bound.

It gets tough and the going is not great,
This path dips and turns, it's not very straight.
Sometimes I wonder where it all will lead,
It's not a lot of fun, being born of His Seed.

The others seem to be having lots of fun,
With their new cars and condos in the sun.
Money in the bank and plans galore,
They don't even consider God's Son – The Door,

To everlasting life and peace,
When will this perfection process cease?
I keep Your ordinances from day to day,
And others don't give a care about what You say.

At times I'm confused and sometimes lost,
I just want so much to please my Boss.
At times I think I'm almost there,
And soon I'll be without a care.

And then the Holy Spirit will show to me,
My inner self - I don't want to see.
That horrible person, so full of pride,
So hateful and selfish, I just can't deny.

That I'm not perfect, not ready yet,
I'm still in the making of that you can bet.
I know that one day when it's all done,
He'll look in His book and I would have won,

By no great works or goodness of my own,
He has perfected me now I'm full grown.
Into His presence now I may stand,
A recreated spirit and brand-new human!

Quest for Salvation

Simply Because You Are Mine

Matthew 7:11; 1 Corinthians 2:9-11; Isaiah 64:4; Psalms 31:19 (KJV)
Scriptural Reference on page 81

Have you ever been blessed by the Lord?

I have, so many times I can't even count.
And it was one day recently that I found out,
A mystery that was hidden from me,
I was blinded, and I didn't really see.

A truth that I had heard many times and should know,
That Jesus loves me, for the Bible tells me so,
But we only really know in part,
And can't truly understand until He expands our heart.

And it was on that day the Lord blessed me well,
My heart was full, and the tears began to swell.
He blessed me with the secrets of my Heart,
Only He and I knew about this part.

You see, I didn't have a revelation of the depth of His love,
And revelation knowledge comes from His Spirit above.

So, one day the Lord spoke softly to me,

"I don't bless you because you are so good,
Or because you always behave as you should,
I bless you because I am true and just and kind,
I bless you simply because you are Mine."

He said,
"Think of how you bless your children at Christmas time,
You plan for weeks for the day when you can make their faces shine.
How much more do I too plan for mine,
Hoping to see their faces shine.

Do you think that I am one who does not feel?
Sometimes I think you don't believe; I am real.
I've been working to prove to you every day,
By providing your needs and wants in every way.

That I love you, not because you are so good,
Or because you always behave as you should,
But because I am true and just and kind,
And Simply Because You Are Mine."

Simply Because You Are Mine

So Be Like Job

Job 1:1, 8-12; 2:1-6; 42:12-13 (KJV)
Scriptural Reference on page 82

Job was a mighty man of God they say,
He made offerings to God, every day.

He was perfect, upright, and very devout,
And God told Satan, to check him out.

His animals and beasts were all carried away,
His servants were killed that terrible day.

A house it fell on his daughters and sons,
Only one was left, to tell all that was done.

Job ripped his clothes and was highly upset,
But he worshipped God, of that you can bet.

He blessed the name of the Lord and did not sin,
It sent Satan running back to the Lord again.

This time Satan set out to do bodily harm,
He thought his next plan would work like a charm.

Job was cursed with sore boils on that day,
But he blessed his God, any ol' way.

Now even Job's wife pressed him the most,
To curse his God, and give up the Ghost.

And even his friends tried to cause him to sin.
But he was full of the Spirit and he did win.

'Cause the Latter End of Job was truly blessed,
For the faith and trust he did possess.

So be like Job in your steadfast Love,
And receive your blessings from God above.

(Rap Style)

So Be Like Job

What's His Face?

Genesis 3:15; John 19:11 (KJV)
Scriptural Reference on page 84

A very long time ago, so the Bible tells,
A foul rotten thing in heaven did dwell.

He was cast from heaven on that fateful day,
He fell to earth, so the scriptures say.

And in his anger, he began to plot and plan,
To get revenge on God's beloved Man.

In the garden of Eden, he did beguile,
While deceiving Adam and Eve all the while.

Then Adam's power over the earth, he did take,
And from that day to this, war on man did make.

But almighty God was just a step ahead,
And sent His Word in the flesh, in man's stead.

In the flesh He came to save you and me,
They crucified Him so all could see.

And that's where the evil one made, his stupid mistake,
For the life of Jesus, he could not take.

'Cause no sin could be found in the Holy One,
The Lamb of God, His beloved Son.

That's when all of his power over you and me,
Was given back to our Savior, you see.

Now he walks around seeking to destroy,
Anyone who believes they are his toy.

But I'm, here to tell that no power exists,
Over those who would only resist,

And claim Jesus as their Savior, the Holy One,
And believe in Him, their life has just begun.

So, put him under foot, when he talks to you,
'Cause you're the Righteousness of God, tried and true.

And He's a thief, a liar, and a big disgrace,
I can't remember his name, you know, "What's his face?"

What's His Face?

Scriptural
References

Bible Character

Luke 22:47, 57, 60; 23:21-34; Mark 15:1, 10-11, 16:1;
Matthew 21:24; 1 Peter 2:9 (KJV)

Luke 22:47 (KJV)

47 And while he yet spake, behold a multitude, and he that was called Judas, one of the twelve, went before them, and drew near unto Jesus to kiss him.

Luke 22:57 (KJV)

57 And he denied him, saying, Woman, I know him not.

Luke 22:60 (KJV)

60 And Peter said, Man, I know not what thou sayest. And immediately, while he yet spake, the cock crew.

Luke 23:21-34 (KJV)

21 But they cried, saying, Crucify him, crucify him.

22 And he said unto them the third time, Why, what evil hath he done? I have found no cause of death in him: I will therefore chastise him, and let him go.

23 And they were instant with loud voices, requiring that he might be crucified. And the voices of them and of the chief priests prevailed.

24 And Pilate gave sentence that it should be as they required.

25 And he released unto them him that for sedition and murder was cast into prison, whom they had desired; but he delivered Jesus to their will.

26 And as they led him away, they laid hold upon one Simon, a Cyrenian, coming out of the country, and on him they laid the cross, that he might bear it after Jesus.

27 And there followed him a great company of people, and of women, which also bewailed and lamented him.

28 But Jesus turning unto them said, Daughters of Jerusalem, weep not for me, but weep for yourselves, and for your children.

[29] For, behold, the days are coming, in the which they shall say, Blessed are the barren, and the wombs that never bare, and the paps which never gave suck.

[30] Then shall they begin to say to the mountains, Fall on us; and to the hills, Cover us.

[31] For if they do these things in a green tree, what shall be done in the dry?

[32] And there were also two other, malefactors, led with him to be put to death.

[33] And when they were come to the place, which is called Calvary, there they crucified him, and the malefactors, one on the right hand, and the other on the left.

[34] Then said Jesus, Father, forgive them; for they know not what they do. And they parted his raiment, and cast lots.

Mark 15:1 (KJV)
[1] And straightway in the morning the chief priests held a consultation with the elders and scribes and the whole council, and bound Jesus, and carried him away, and delivered him to Pilate.

Mark 15:10-11 (KJV)
[10] For he knew that the chief priests had delivered him for envy.
[11] But the chief priests moved the people, that he should rather release Barabbas unto them.

Mark 16:1 (KJV)
[1] And when the sabbath was past, Mary Magdalene, and Mary the mother of James, and Salome, had bought sweet spices, that they might come and anoint him.

Matthew 21:24

24 And Jesus answered and said unto them, I also will ask you one thing, which if ye tell me, I in like wise will tell you by what authority I do these things.

1 Peter 2:9 (KJV)

9 But ye are a chosen generation, a royal priesthood, an holy nation, a peculiar people; that ye should shew forth the praises of him who hath called you out of darkness into his marvellous light;

Birthright

Genesis 27:1-46, 29:16-20, 23-28 (KJV)

Genesis 27:1-46 (KJV)

¹ And it came to pass, that when Isaac was old, and his eyes were dim, so that he could not see, he called Esau his eldest son, and said unto him, My son: and he said unto him, Behold, here am I.

² And he said, Behold now, I am old, I know not the day of my death:

³ Now therefore take, I pray thee, thy weapons, thy quiver and thy bow, and go out to the field, and take me some venison;

⁴ And make me savoury meat, such as I love, and bring it to me, that I may eat; that my soul may bless thee before I die.

⁵ And Rebekah heard when Isaac spake to Esau his son. And Esau went to the field to hunt for venison, and to bring it.

⁶ And Rebekah spake unto Jacob her son, saying, Behold, I heard thy father speak unto Esau thy brother, saying,

⁷ Bring me venison, and make me savoury meat, that I may eat, and bless thee before the LORD before my death.

⁸ Now therefore, my son, obey my voice according to that which I command thee.

⁹ Go now to the flock, and fetch me from thence two good kids of the goats; and I will make them savoury meat for thy father, such as he loveth:

¹⁰ And thou shalt bring it to thy father, that he may eat, and that he may bless thee before his death.

¹¹ And Jacob said to Rebekah his mother, Behold, Esau my brother is a hairy man, and I am a smooth man:

¹² My father peradventure will feel me, and I shall seem to him as a deceiver; and I shall bring a curse upon me, and not a blessing.

¹³ And his mother said unto him, Upon me be thy curse, my son: only obey my voice, and go fetch me them.

¹⁴ And he went, and fetched, and brought them to his mother: and his mother made savoury meat, such as his father loved.

15 And Rebekah took goodly raiment of her eldest son Esau, which were with her in the house, and put them upon Jacob her younger son:

16 And she put the skins of the kids of the goats upon his hands, and upon the smooth of his neck:

17 And she gave the savoury meat and the bread, which she had prepared, into the hand of her son Jacob.

18 And he came unto his father, and said, My father: and he said, Here am I; who art thou, my son?

19 And Jacob said unto his father, I am Esau thy first born; I have done according as thou badest me: arise, I pray thee, sit and eat of my venison, that thy soul may bless me.

20 And Isaac said unto his son, How is it that thou hast found it so quickly, my son? And he said, Because the LORD thy God brought it to me.

21 And Isaac said unto Jacob, Come near, I pray thee, that I may feel thee, my son, whether thou be my very son Esau or not.

22 And Jacob went near unto Isaac his father; and he felt him, and said, The voice is Jacob's voice, but the hands are the hands of Esau.

23 And he discerned him not, because his hands were hairy, as his brother Esau's hands: so he blessed him.

24 And he said, Art thou my very son Esau? And he said, I am.

25 And he said, Bring it near to me, and I will eat of my son's venison, that my soul may bless thee. And he brought it near to him, and he did eat: and he brought him wine and he drank.

26 And his father Isaac said unto him, Come near now, and kiss me, my son.

²⁷ And he came near, and kissed him: and he smelled the smell of his raiment, and blessed him, and said, See, the smell of my son is as the smell of a field which the LORD hath blessed:

²⁸ Therefore God give thee of the dew of heaven, and the fatness of the earth, and plenty of corn and wine:

²⁹ Let people serve thee, and nations bow down to thee: be lord over thy brethren, and let thy mother's sons bow down to thee: cursed be every one that curseth thee, and blessed be he that blesseth thee.

³⁰ And it came to pass, as soon as Isaac had made an end of blessing Jacob, and Jacob was yet scarce gone out from the presence of Isaac his father, that Esau his brother came in from his hunting.

³¹ And he also had made savoury meat, and brought it unto his father, and said unto his father, Let my father arise, and eat of his son's venison, that thy soul may bless me.

³² And Isaac his father said unto him, Who art thou? And he said, I am thy son, thy firstborn Esau.

³³ And Isaac trembled very exceedingly, and said, Who? where is he that hath taken venison, and brought it me, and I have eaten of all before thou camest, and have blessed him? yea, and he shall be blessed.

³⁴ And when Esau heard the words of his father, he cried with a great and exceeding bitter cry, and said unto his father, Bless me, even me also, O my father.

³⁵ And he said, Thy brother came with subtilty, and hath taken away thy blessing.

³⁶ And he said, Is not he rightly named Jacob? for he hath supplanted me these two times: he took away my birthright; and, behold, now he hath taken away my blessing. And he said, Hast thou not reserved a blessing for me?

37 And Isaac answered and said unto Esau, Behold, I have made him thy lord, and all his brethren have I given to him for servants; and with corn and wine have I sustained him: and what shall I do now unto thee, my son?

38 And Esau said unto his father, Hast thou but one blessing, my father? bless me, even me also, O my father. And Esau lifted up his voice, and wept.

39 And Isaac his father answered and said unto him, Behold, thy dwelling shall be the fatness of the earth, and of the dew of heaven from above;

40 And by thy sword shalt thou live, and shalt serve thy brother; and it shall come to pass when thou shalt have the dominion, that thou shalt break his yoke from off thy neck.

41 And Esau hated Jacob because of the blessing wherewith his father blessed him: and Esau said in his heart, The days of mourning for my father are at hand; then will I slay my brother Jacob.

42 And these words of Esau her elder son were told to Rebekah: and she sent and called Jacob her younger son, and said unto him, Behold, thy brother Esau, as touching thee, doth comfort himself, purposing to kill thee.

43 Now therefore, my son, obey my voice; arise, flee thou to Laban my brother to Haran;

44 And tarry with him a few days, until thy brother's fury turn away;

45 Until thy brother's anger turn away from thee, and he forget that which thou hast done to him: then I will send, and fetch thee from thence: why should I be deprived also of you both in one day?

46 And Rebekah said to Isaac, I am weary of my life because of the daughters of Heth: if Jacob take a wife of the daughters of Heth, such as these which are of the daughters of the land, what good shall my life do me?

Genesis 29:16-20 (KJV)

16 And Laban had two daughters: the name of the elder was Leah, and the name of the younger was Rachel.

17 Leah was tender eyed; but Rachel was beautiful and well favoured.

18 And Jacob loved Rachel; and said, I will serve thee seven years for Rachel thy younger daughter.

19 And Laban said, It is better that I give her to thee, than that I should give her to another man: abide with me.

20 And Jacob served seven years for Rachel; and they seemed unto him but a few days, for the love he had to her.

Genesis 29:23-28 (KJV)

23 And it came to pass in the evening, that he took Leah his daughter, and brought her to him; and he went in unto her.

24 And Laban gave unto his daughter Leah Zilpah his maid for an handmaid.

25 And it came to pass, that in the morning, behold, it was Leah: and he said to Laban, What is this thou hast done unto me? did not I serve with thee for Rachel? wherefore then hast thou beguiled me?

26 And Laban said, It must not be so done in our country, to give the younger before the firstborn.

27 Fulfil her week, and we will give thee this also for the service which thou shalt serve with me yet seven other years.

28 And Jacob did so, and fulfilled her week: and he gave him Rachel his daughter to wife also.

Bringing His Family Out

Genesis 3:22-24; Mark 1:14-15; 1 Peter 2:9; 1 Corinthians 2:12; Ephesians 1:3-6; Acts 2:17; Matthew 24:21-22; Hebrews 10:38 (KJV)

Genesis 3:22-24 (KJV)

22 And the LORD God said, Behold, the man is become as one of us, to know good and evil: and now, lest he put forth his hand, and take also of the tree of life, and eat, and live for ever:

23 Therefore the LORD God sent him forth from the garden of Eden, to till the ground from whence he was taken.

24 So he drove out the man; and he placed at the east of the garden of Eden Cherubims, and a flaming sword which turned every way, to keep the way of the tree of life.

Mark 1:14-15 (KJV)

14 Now after that John was put in prison, Jesus came into Galilee, preaching the gospel of the kingdom of God,

15 And saying, The time is fulfilled, and the kingdom of God is at hand: repent ye, and believe the gospel.

1 Peter 2:9 (KJV)

9 But ye are a chosen generation, a royal priesthood, an holy nation, a peculiar people; that ye should shew forth the praises of him who hath called you out of darkness into his marvellous light;

1 Corinthians 2:12 (KJV)

12 Now we have received, not the spirit of the world, but the spirit which is of God; that we might know the things that are freely given to us of God.

Ephesians 1:3-6 (KJV)

3 Blessed be the God and Father of our Lord Jesus Christ, who hath blessed us with all spiritual blessings in heavenly places in Christ:

4 According as he hath chosen us in him before the foundation of the world, that we should be holy and without blame before him in love:

5 Having predestinated us unto the adoption of children by Jesus Christ to himself, according to the good pleasure of his will,
6 To the praise of the glory of his grace, wherein he hath made us accepted in the beloved.

Acts 2:17 (KJV)
17 And it shall come to pass in the last days, saith God, I will pour out of my Spirit upon all flesh: and your sons and your daughters shall prophesy, and your young men shall see visions, and your old men shall dream dreams:

Matthew 24:21-22 (KJV)
21 For then shall be great tribulation, such as was not since the beginning of the world to this time, no, nor ever shall be.
22 And except those days should be shortened, there should no flesh be saved: but for the elect's sake those days shall be shortened.

Hebrews 10:38 (KJV)
38 Now the just shall live by faith: but if any man draw back, my soul shall have no pleasure in him.

Bringing His Family Out   Scripture References

Dr. Lydia A. Woods

The Day of His Birth

Genesis 1:26-27; Luke 2:6-14 (KJV)

Genesis 1:26-27 (KJV)

26 And God said, Let us make man in our image, after our likeness: and let them have dominion over the fish of the sea, and over the fowl of the air, and over the cattle, and over all the earth, and over every creeping thing that creepeth upon the earth.

27 So God created man in his own image, in the image of God created he him; male and female created he them.

Luke 2:6-14 (KJV)

6 And so it was, that, while they were there, the days were accomplished that she should be delivered.

7 And she brought forth her firstborn son, and wrapped him in swaddling clothes, and laid him in a manger; because there was no room for them in the inn.

8 And there were in the same country shepherds abiding in the field, keeping watch over their flock by night.

9 And, lo, the angel of the Lord came upon them, and the glory of the Lord shone round about them: and they were sore afraid.

10 And the angel said unto them, Fear not: for, behold, I bring you good tidings of great joy, which shall be to all people.

11 For unto you is born this day in the city of David a Saviour, which is Christ the Lord.

12 And this shall be a sign unto you; Ye shall find the babe wrapped in swaddling clothes, lying in a manger.

13 And suddenly there was with the angel a multitude of the heavenly host praising God, and saying,

14 Glory to God in the highest, and on earth peace, good will toward men.

Scripture References   The Day of His Birth

Doin' the Israelite

Exodus 11:2, 13:21; 14:27-28, 16:2-3,12, 17:2-4 (KJV)

Exodus 11:2 (KJV)

2 Speak now in the ears of the people, and let every man borrow of his neighbour, and every woman of her neighbour, jewels of silver and jewels of gold.

Exodus 13:21 (KJV)

21 And the LORD went before them by day in a pillar of a cloud, to lead them the way; and by night in a pillar of fire, to give them light; to go by day and night:

Exodus 14:27-28 (KJV)

27 And Moses stretched forth his hand over the sea, and the sea returned to his strength when the morning appeared; and the Egyptians fled against it; and the LORD overthrew the Egyptians in the midst of the sea.

28 And the waters returned, and covered the chariots, and the horsemen, and all the host of Pharaoh that came into the sea after them; there remained not so much as one of them.

Exodus 16:2-3 (KJV)

2 And the whole congregation of the children of Israel murmured against Moses and Aaron in the wilderness:

3 And the children of Israel said unto them, Would to God we had died by the hand of the LORD in the land of Egypt, when we sat by the flesh pots, and when we did eat bread to the full; for ye have brought us forth into this wilderness, to kill this whole assembly with hunger.

Exodus 16:12 (KJV)

12 I have heard the murmurings of the children of Israel: speak unto them, saying, At even ye shall eat flesh, and in the morning ye shall be filled with bread; and ye shall know that I am the LORD your God.

Exodus 17:2-4 (KJV)

2 Wherefore the people did chide with Moses, and said, Give us water that we may drink. And Moses said unto them, Why chide ye with me? wherefore do ye tempt the LORD?

3 And the people thirsted there for water; and the people murmured against Moses, and said, Wherefore is this that thou hast brought us up out of Egypt, to kill us and our children and our cattle with thirst?

4 And Moses cried unto the LORD, saying, What shall I do unto this people? they be almost ready to stone me.

Get a Testimony

Luke 4:18-19; James 1:2-4 (KJV)

Luke 4:18-19 (KJV)

18 The Spirit of the Lord is upon me, because he hath anointed me to preach the gospel to the poor; he hath sent me to heal the brokenhearted, to preach deliverance to the captives, and recovering of sight to the blind, to set at liberty them that are bruised,
19 To preach the acceptable year of the Lord.

James 1:2-4 (KJV)

2 My brethren, count it all joy when ye fall into divers temptations;
3 Knowing this, that the trying of your faith worketh patience.
4 But let patience have her perfect work, that ye may be perfect and entire, wanting nothing.

Getting to Know You

Proverbs 1:7, 2:1,3:1-4 (KJV)

Proverbs 1:7 (KJV)

7 The fear of the LORD is the beginning of knowledge: but fools despise wisdom and instruction.

Proverbs 2:1 (KJV)

1My son, if thou wilt receive my words, and hide my commandments with thee;

Proverbs 3:1-4 (KJV)

1My son, forget not my law; but let thine heart keep my commandments:
2 For length of days, and long life, and peace, shall they add to thee.
3 Let not mercy and truth forsake thee: bind them about thy neck; write them upon the table of thine heart:
4 So shalt thou find favour and good understanding in the sight of God and man.

Good News

*1 Corinthians 15:3, 15:52; Mark 13:24-27; Revelation 1:7, 19:7-9;
20:1-3, 21:1-5 (KJV)*

1 Corinthians 15:3 (KJV)

3 For I delivered unto you first of all that which I also received, how that Christ died for our sins according to the scriptures;

1 Corinthians 15:52 (KJV)

52 In a moment, in the twinkling of an eye, at the last trump: for the trumpet shall sound, and the dead shall be raised incorruptible, and we shall be changed.

Mark 13:24-27 (KJV)

24 But in those days, after that tribulation, the sun shall be darkened, and the moon shall not give her light,

25 And the stars of heaven shall fall, and the powers that are in heaven shall be shaken.

26 And then shall they see the Son of man coming in the clouds with great power and glory.

27 And then shall he send his angels, and shall gather together his elect from the four winds, from the uttermost part of the earth to the uttermost part of heaven.

Revelation 1:7 (KJV)

7 Behold, he cometh with clouds; and every eye shall see him, and they also which pierced him: and all kindreds of the earth shall wail because of him. Even so, Amen.

Revelation 19:7-9 (KJV)

7 Let us be glad and rejoice, and give honour to him: for the marriage of the Lamb is come, and his wife hath made herself ready.

8 And to her was granted that she should be arrayed in fine linen, clean and white: for the fine linen is the righteousness of saints.

[9] And he saith unto me, Write, Blessed are they which are called unto the marriage supper of the Lamb. And he saith unto me, These are the true sayings of God.

Revelation 20:1-3 (KJV)

[1] And I saw an angel come down from heaven, having the key of the bottomless pit and a great chain in his hand.

[2] And he laid hold on the dragon, that old serpent, which is the Devil, and Satan, and bound him a thousand years,

[3] And cast him into the bottomless pit, and shut him up, and set a seal upon him, that he should deceive the nations no more, till the thousand years should be fulfilled: and after that he must be loosed a little season.

Revelation 21:1-5 (KJV)

[1] And I saw a new heaven and a new earth: for the first heaven and the first earth were passed away; and there was no more sea.

[2] And I John saw the holy city, new Jerusalem, coming down from God out of heaven, prepared as a bride adorned for her husband.

[3] And I heard a great voice out of heaven saying, Behold, the tabernacle of God is with men, and he will dwell with them, and they shall be his people, and God himself shall be with them, and be their God.

[4] And God shall wipe away all tears from their eyes; and there shall be no more death, neither sorrow, nor crying, neither shall there be any more pain: for the former things are passed away.

[5] And he that sat upon the throne said, Behold, I make all things new. And he said unto me, Write: for these words are true and faithful.

Good News II

Mark 16:15-18; Revelation 2:1-29, 3:1-22 (KJV)

Mark 16:15-18 (KJV)

¹⁵ And he said unto them, Go ye into all the world, and preach the gospel to every creature.

¹⁶ He that believeth and is baptized shall be saved; but he that believeth not shall be damned.

¹⁷ And these signs shall follow them that believe; In my name shall they cast out devils; they shall speak with new tongues;

¹⁸ They shall take up serpents; and if they drink any deadly thing, it shall not hurt them; they shall lay hands on the sick, and they shall recover.

Revelation 2:1-29 (KJV)

¹ Unto the angel of the church of Ephesus write; These things saith he that holdeth the seven stars in his right hand, who walketh in the midst of the seven golden candlesticks;

² I know thy works, and thy labour, and thy patience, and how thou canst not bear them which are evil: and thou hast tried them which say they are apostles, and are not, and hast found them liars:

³ And hast borne, and hast patience, and for my name's sake hast laboured, and hast not fainted.

⁴ Nevertheless I have somewhat against thee, because thou hast left thy first love.

⁵ Remember therefore from whence thou art fallen, and repent, and do the first works; or else I will come unto thee quickly, and will remove thy candlestick out of his place, except thou repent.

⁶ But this thou hast, that thou hatest the deeds of the Nicolaitanes, which I also hate.

⁷ He that hath an ear, let him hear what the Spirit saith unto the churches; To him that overcometh will I give to eat of the tree of life, which is in the midst of the paradise of God.

8 And unto the angel of the church in Smyrna write; These things saith the first and the last, which was dead, and is alive;

9 I know thy works, and tribulation, and poverty, (but thou art rich) and I know the blasphemy of them which say they are Jews, and are not, but are the synagogue of Satan.

10 Fear none of those things which thou shalt suffer: behold, the devil shall cast some of you into prison, that ye may be tried; and ye shall have tribulation ten days: be thou faithful unto death, and I will give thee a crown of life.

11 He that hath an ear, let him hear what the Spirit saith unto the churches; He that overcometh shall not be hurt of the second death.

12 And to the angel of the church in Pergamos write; These things saith he which hath the sharp sword with two edges;

13 I know thy works, and where thou dwellest, even where Satan's seat is: and thou holdest fast my name, and hast not denied my faith, even in those days wherein Antipas was my faithful martyr, who was slain among you, where Satan dwelleth.

14 But I have a few things against thee, because thou hast there them that hold the doctrine of Balaam, who taught Balac to cast a stumblingblock before the children of Israel, to eat things sacrificed unto idols, and to commit fornication.

15 So hast thou also them that hold the doctrine of the Nicolaitanes, which thing I hate.

16 Repent; or else I will come unto thee quickly, and will fight against them with the sword of my mouth.

17 He that hath an ear, let him hear what the Spirit saith unto the churches; To him that overcometh will I give to eat of the hidden manna, and will give him a white stone, and in the stone a new name written, which no man knoweth saving he that receiveth it.

[18] And unto the angel of the church in Thyatira write; These things saith the Son of God, who hath his eyes like unto a flame of fire, and his feet are like fine brass;

[19] I know thy works, and charity, and service, and faith, and thy patience, and thy works; and the last to be more than the first.

[20] Notwithstanding I have a few things against thee, because thou sufferest that woman Jezebel, which calleth herself a prophetess, to teach and to seduce my servants to commit fornication, and to eat things sacrificed unto idols.

[21] And I gave her space to repent of her fornication; and she repented not.

[22] Behold, I will cast her into a bed, and them that commit adultery with her into great tribulation, except they repent of their deeds.

[23] And I will kill her children with death; and all the churches shall know that I am he which searcheth the reins and hearts: and I will give unto every one of you according to your works.

[24] But unto you I say, and unto the rest in Thyatira, as many as have not this doctrine, and which have not known the depths of Satan, as they speak; I will put upon you none other burden.

[25] But that which ye have already hold fast till I come.

[26] And he that overcometh, and keepeth my works unto the end, to him will I give power over the nations:

[27] And he shall rule them with a rod of iron; as the vessels of a potter shall they be broken to shivers: even as I received of my Father.

[28] And I will give him the morning star.

[29] He that hath an ear, let him hear what the Spirit saith unto the churches.

Revelation 3:1-22 (KJV)

[1] And unto the angel of the church in Sardis write; These things saith he that hath the seven Spirits of God, and the seven stars; I know thy works, that thou hast a name that thou livest, and art dead.

[2] Be watchful, and strengthen the things which remain, that are ready to die: for I have not found thy works perfect before God.

[3] Remember therefore how thou hast received and heard, and hold fast, and repent. If therefore thou shalt not watch, I will come on thee as a thief, and thou shalt not know what hour I will come upon thee.

[4] Thou hast a few names even in Sardis which have not defiled their garments; and they shall walk with me in white: for they are worthy.

[5] He that overcometh, the same shall be clothed in white raiment; and I will not blot out his name out of the book of life, but I will confess his name before my Father, and before his angels.

[6] He that hath an ear, let him hear what the Spirit saith unto the churches.

[7] And to the angel of the church in Philadelphia write; These things saith he that is holy, he that is true, he that hath the key of David, he that openeth, and no man shutteth; and shutteth, and no man openeth;

[8] I know thy works: behold, I have set before thee an open door, and no man can shut it: for thou hast a little strength, and hast kept my word, and hast not denied my name.

[9] Behold, I will make them of the synagogue of Satan, which say they are Jews, and are not, but do lie; behold, I will make them to come and worship before thy feet, and to know that I have loved thee.

[10] Because thou hast kept the word of my patience, I also will keep thee from the hour of temptation, which shall come upon all the world, to try them that dwell upon the earth.

[11] Behold, I come quickly: hold that fast which thou hast, that no man take thy crown.

[12] Him that overcometh will I make a pillar in the temple of my God, and he shall go no more out: and I will write upon him the name of my God, and the name of the city of my God, which is new Jerusalem, which cometh down out of heaven from my God: and I will write upon him my new name.

[13] He that hath an ear, let him hear what the Spirit saith unto the churches.

[14] And unto the angel of the church of the Laodiceans write; These things saith the Amen, the faithful and true witness, the beginning of the creation of God;

[15] I know thy works, that thou art neither cold nor hot: I would thou wert cold or hot.

[16] So then because thou art lukewarm, and neither cold nor hot, I will spue thee out of my mouth.

[17] Because thou sayest, I am rich, and increased with goods, and have need of nothing; and knowest not that thou art wretched, and miserable, and poor, and blind, and naked:

[18] I counsel thee to buy of me gold tried in the fire, that thou mayest be rich; and white raiment, that thou mayest be clothed, and that the shame of thy nakedness do not appear; and anoint thine eyes with eyesalve, that thou mayest see.

[19] As many as I love, I rebuke and chasten: be zealous therefore, and repent.

[20] Behold, I stand at the door, and knock: if any man hear my voice, and open the door, I will come in to him, and will sup with him, and he with me.

[21] To him that overcometh will I grant to sit with me in my throne, even as I also overcame, and am set down with my Father in his throne. [22] He that hath an ear, let him hear what the Spirit saith unto the churches.

It's Adoption Time

Galatians 4:5-7; Ephesians 1:4-5 (KJV)

Galatians 4:5-7 (KJV)

5 To redeem them that were under the law, that we might receive the adoption of sons.

6 And because ye are sons, God hath sent forth the Spirit of his Son into your hearts, crying, Abba, Father.

7 Wherefore thou art no more a servant, but a son; and if a son, then an heir of God through Christ.

Ephesians 1:4-5 (KJV)

4 According as he hath chosen us in him before the foundation of the world, that we should be holy and without blame before him in love:

5 Having predestinated us unto the adoption of children by Jesus Christ to himself, according to the good pleasure of his will,

It's War!

Ephesians 6:10-17 (KJV)

Ephesians 6:10-17 (KJV)

[10] Finally, my brethren, be strong in the Lord, and in the power of his might.

[11] Put on the whole armour of God, that ye may be able to stand against the wiles of the devil.

[12] For we wrestle not against flesh and blood, but against principalities, against powers, against the rulers of the darkness of this world, against spiritual wickedness in high places.

[13] Wherefore take unto you the whole armour of God, that ye may be able to withstand in the evil day, and having done all, to stand.

[14] Stand therefore, having your loins girt about with truth, and having on the breastplate of righteousness;

[15] And your feet shod with the preparation of the gospel of peace;

[16] Above all, taking the shield of faith, wherewith ye shall be able to quench all the fiery darts of the wicked.

[17] And take the helmet of salvation, and the sword of the Spirit, which is the word of God:

Joseph

Genesis 37:2-5, 9, 15, 31-35, 41:41-43, 45:1-5 (KJV)

Genesis 37:2-5 (KJV)

2 These are the generations of Jacob. Joseph, being seventeen years old, was feeding the flock with his brethren; and the lad was with the sons of Bilhah, and with the sons of Zilpah, his father's wives: and Joseph brought unto his father their evil report.
3 Now Israel loved Joseph more than all his children, because he was the son of his old age: and he made him a coat of many colours.
4 And when his brethren saw that their father loved him more than all his brethren, they hated him, and could not speak peaceably unto him.
5 And Joseph dreamed a dream, and he told it his brethren: and they hated him yet the more.

Genesis 37:9 (KJV)

9 And he dreamed yet another dream, and told it his brethren, and said, Behold, I have dreamed a dream more; and, behold, the sun and the moon and the eleven stars made obeisance to me.

Genesis 37:15 (KJV)

15 And a certain man found him, and, behold, he was wandering in the field: and the man asked him, saying, What seekest thou?

Genesis 37:31-35 (KJV)

31 And they took Joseph's coat, and killed a kid of the goats, and dipped the coat in the blood;
32 And they sent the coat of many colours, and they brought it to their father; and said, This have we found: know now whether it be thy son's coat or no.
33 And he knew it, and said, It is my son's coat; an evil beast hath devoured him; Joseph is without doubt rent in pieces.
34 And Jacob rent his clothes, and put sackcloth upon his loins, and mourned for his son many days.

35 And all his sons and all his daughters rose up to comfort him; but he refused to be comforted; and he said, For I will go down into the grave unto my son mourning. Thus his father wept for him.

Genesis 41:41-43 (KJV)

41 And Pharaoh said unto Joseph, See, I have set thee over all the land of Egypt.

42 And Pharaoh took off his ring from his hand, and put it upon Joseph's hand, and arrayed him in vestures of fine linen, and put a gold chain about his neck;

43 And he made him to ride in the second chariot which he had; and they cried before him, Bow the knee: and he made him ruler over all the land of Egypt.

Genesis 45:1-5 (KJV)

1Then Joseph could not refrain himself before all them that stood by him; and he cried, Cause every man to go out from me. And there stood no man with him, while Joseph made himself known unto his brethren.

2 And he wept aloud: and the Egyptians and the house of Pharaoh heard.

3 And Joseph said unto his brethren, I am Joseph; doth my father yet live? And his brethren could not answer him; for they were troubled at his presence.

4 And Joseph said unto his brethren, Come near to me, I pray you. And they came near. And he said, I am Joseph your brother, whom ye sold into Egypt.

5 Now therefore be not grieved, nor angry with yourselves, that ye sold me hither: for God did send me before you to preserve life.

Just Do It!

Mark 16:15-20 (KJV)

Mark 16:15-20 (KJV)

15 And he said unto them, Go ye into all the world, and preach the gospel to every creature.

16 He that believeth and is baptized shall be saved; but he that believeth not shall be damned.

17 And these signs shall follow them that believe; In my name shall they cast out devils; they shall speak with new tongues;

18 They shall take up serpents; and if they drink any deadly thing, it shall not hurt them; they shall lay hands on the sick, and they shall recover.

19 So then after the Lord had spoken unto them, he was received up into heaven, and sat on the right hand of God.

20 And they went forth, and preached every where, the Lord working with them, and confirming the word with signs following. Amen.

Master of Masters

Matthew 4:1, 4:19, 5:1, 7:29, 8:26, 11:5; Luke 8:43-48;
John 2:1-11, 11:43-44 (KJV)

Matthew 4:1 (KJV)
1 Then was Jesus led up of the Spirit into the wilderness to be tempted of the devil.

Matthew 4:19 (KJV)
19 And he saith unto them, Follow me, and I will make you fishers of men.

Matthew 5:1 (KJV)
1 And seeing the multitudes, he went up into a mountain: and when he was set, his disciples came unto him:

Matthew 7:29 (KJV)
29 For he taught them as one having authority, and not as the scribes.

Matthew 8:26 (KJV)
26 And he saith unto them, Why are ye fearful, O ye of little faith? Then he arose, and rebuked the winds and the sea; and there was a great calm.

Matthew 11:5 (KJV)
5 The blind receive their sight, and the lame walk, the lepers are cleansed, and the deaf hear, the dead are raised up, and the poor have the gospel preached to them.

Luke 8:43-48 (KJV)
43 And a woman having an issue of blood twelve years, which had spent all her living upon physicians, neither could be healed of any,
44 Came behind him, and touched the border of his garment: and immediately her issue of blood stanched.
45 And Jesus said, Who touched me? When all denied, Peter and they that were with him said, Master, the multitude throng thee and press thee, and sayest thou, Who touched me?

⁴⁶ And Jesus said, Somebody hath touched me: for I perceive that virtue is gone out of me.

⁴⁷ And when the woman saw that she was not hid, she came trembling, and falling down before him, she declared unto him before all the people for what cause she had touched him, and how she was healed immediately.

⁴⁸ And he said unto her, Daughter, be of good comfort: thy faith hath made thee whole; go in peace.

John 2:1-11 (KJV)

¹ And the third day there was a marriage in Cana of Galilee; and the mother of Jesus was there:

² And both Jesus was called, and his disciples, to the marriage.

³ And when they wanted wine, the mother of Jesus saith unto him, They have no wine.

⁴ Jesus saith unto her, Woman, what have I to do with thee? mine hour is not yet come.

⁵ His mother saith unto the servants, Whatsoever he saith unto you, do it.

⁶ And there were set there six waterpots of stone, after the manner of the purifying of the Jews, containing two or three firkins apiece.

⁷ Jesus saith unto them, Fill the waterpots with water. And they filled them up to the brim.

⁸ And he saith unto them, Draw out now, and bear unto the governor of the feast. And they bare it.

⁹ When the ruler of the feast had tasted the water that was made wine, and knew not whence it was: (but the servants which drew the water knew;) the governor of the feast called the bridegroom,

[10] And saith unto him, Every man at the beginning doth set forth good wine; and when men have well drunk, then that which is worse: but thou hast kept the good wine until now.

[11] This beginning of miracles did Jesus in Cana of Galilee, and manifested forth his glory; and his disciples believed on him.

John 11:43-44 (KJV)

[43] And when he thus had spoken, he cried with a loud voice, Lazarus, come forth.

[44] And he that was dead came forth, bound hand and foot with graveclothes: and his face was bound about with a napkin. Jesus saith unto them, Loose him, and let him go.

No Abundance in the Wilderness

Matthew 4:1-11 (KJV)

Matthew 4:1-11 (KJV)

¹Then was Jesus led up of the Spirit into the wilderness to be tempted of the devil.

² And when he had fasted forty days and forty nights, he was afterward an hungred.

³ And when the tempter came to him, he said, If thou be the Son of God, command that these stones be made bread.

⁴ But he answered and said, It is written, Man shall not live by bread alone, but by every word that proceedeth out of the mouth of God.

⁵ Then the devil taketh him up into the holy city, and setteth him on a pinnacle of the temple,

⁶ And saith unto him, If thou be the Son of God, cast thyself down: for it is written, He shall give his angels charge concerning thee: and in their hands they shall bear thee up, lest at any time thou dash thy foot against a stone.

⁷ Jesus said unto him, It is written again, Thou shalt not tempt the Lord thy God.

⁸ Again, the devil taketh him up into an exceeding high mountain, and sheweth him all the kingdoms of the world, and the glory of them;

⁹ And saith unto him, All these things will I give thee, if thou wilt fall down and worship me.

¹⁰ Then saith Jesus unto him, Get thee hence, Satan: for it is written, Thou shalt worship the Lord thy God, and him only shalt thou serve.

¹¹ Then the devil leaveth him, and, behold, angels came and ministered unto him.

Dr. Lydia A. Woods

Put It All On!

Ephesians 6:11-17 (KJV)

Ephesians 6:11-17 (KJV)

11 Put on the whole armour of God, that ye may be able to stand against the wiles of the devil.

12 For we wrestle not against flesh and blood, but against principalities, against powers, against the rulers of the darkness of this world, against spiritual wickedness in high places.

13 Wherefore take unto you the whole armour of God, that ye may be able to withstand in the evil day, and having done all, to stand.

14 Stand therefore, having your loins girt about with truth, and having on the breastplate of righteousness;

15 And your feet shod with the preparation of the gospel of peace;

16 Above all, taking the shield of faith, wherewith ye shall be able to quench all the fiery darts of the wicked.

17 And take the helmet of salvation, and the sword of the Spirit, which is the word of God:

Quest for Salvation

Malachi 3:13-18 (KJV)

Malachi 3:13-18 (KJV)

13 Your words have been stout against me, saith the LORD. Yet ye say, What have we spoken so much against thee?

14 Ye have said, It is vain to serve God: and what profit is it that we have kept his ordinance, and that we have walked mournfully before the LORD of hosts?

15 And now we call the proud happy; yea, they that work wickedness are set up; yea, they that tempt God are even delivered.

16 Then they that feared the LORD spake often one to another: and the LORD hearkened, and heard it, and a book of remembrance was written before him for them that feared the LORD, and that thought upon his name.

17 And they shall be mine, saith the LORD of hosts, in that day when I make up my jewels; and I will spare them, as a man spareth his own son that serveth him.

18 Then shall ye return, and discern between the righteous and the wicked, between him that serveth God and him that serveth him not.

Simply Because You Are Mine

Matthew 7:11; 1 Corinthians 2:9-11; Isaiah 64:4; Psalms 31:19 (KJV)

Matthew 7:11 (KJV)

11 If ye then, being evil, know how to give good gifts unto your children, how much more shall your Father which is in heaven give good things to them that ask him?

1 Corinthians 2:9-11 (KJV)

9 But as it is written, Eye hath not seen, nor ear heard, neither have entered into the heart of man, the things which God hath prepared for them that love him.

10 But God hath revealed them unto us by his Spirit: for the Spirit searcheth all things, yea, the deep things of God.

11 For what man knoweth the things of a man, save the spirit of man which is in him? even so the things of God knoweth no man, but the Spirit of God.

Isaiah 64:4 (KJV)

4 For since the beginning of the world men have not heard, nor perceived by the ear, neither hath the eye seen, O God, beside thee, what he hath prepared for him that waiteth for him.

Psalms 31:19 (KJV)

19 Oh how great is thy goodness, which thou hast laid up for them that fear thee; which thou hast wrought for them that trust in thee before the sons of men!

So Be Like Job

Job 1:1, 8-12; 2:1-6; 42:12-13 (KJV)

Job 1:1 (KJV)

1 There was a man in the land of Uz, whose name was Job; and that man was perfect and upright, and one that feared God, and eschewed evil.

Job 1:8-12 (KJV)

8 And the Lord said unto Satan, Hast thou considered my servant Job, that there is none like him in the earth, a perfect and an upright man, one that feareth God, and escheweth evil?

9 Then Satan answered the Lord, and said, Doth Job fear God for nought?

10 Hast not thou made an hedge about him, and about his house, and about all that he hath on every side? thou hast blessed the work of his hands, and his substance is increased in the land.

11 But put forth thine hand now, and touch all that he hath, and he will curse thee to thy face.

12 And the Lord said unto Satan, Behold, all that he hath is in thy power; only upon himself put not forth thine hand. So Satan went forth from the presence of the Lord.

Job 2:1-6 (KJV)

1 Again there was a day when the sons of God came to present themselves before the Lord, and Satan came also among them to present himself before the Lord.

2 And the Lord said unto Satan, From whence comest thou? And Satan answered the Lord, and said, From going to and fro in the earth, and from walking up and down in it.

[3] And the Lord said unto Satan, Hast thou considered my servant Job, that there is none like him in the earth, a perfect and an upright man, one that feareth God, and escheweth evil? and still he holdeth fast his integrity, although thou movedst me against him, to destroy him without cause.

[4] And Satan answered the Lord, and said, Skin for skin, yea, all that a man hath will he give for his life.

[5] But put forth thine hand now, and touch his bone and his flesh, and he will curse thee to thy face.

[6] And the Lord said unto Satan, Behold, he is in thine hand; but save his life.

Job 42:12-13 (KJV)

[12] So the Lord blessed the latter end of Job more than his beginning: for he had fourteen thousand sheep, and six thousand camels, and a thousand yoke of oxen, and a thousand she asses.

[13] He had also seven sons and three daughters.

What's His Face?

Genesis 3:15; John 19:11 (KJV)

Genesis 3:15 (KJV)

15 And I will put enmity between thee and the woman, and between thy seed and her seed; it shall bruise thy head, and thou shalt bruise his heel.

John 19:11 (KJV)

11 Jesus answered, Thou couldest have no power at all against me, except it were given thee from above: therefore he that delivered me unto thee hath the greater sin.

Scriptural Index